Mini

JUNIOR SCHOOL ESSAYS

ARVIND NANDA
M.A.(Eng.), M.Ed.

MINI BOOKS
PUBLISHERS

JUNIOR SCHOOL ESSAYS

First Published : 1999
Sixteenth Revised Edition : 2011

Price : ₹ 35.00 only

Published by :
MINI BOOKS
(An Imprint of Chaudhary Book Company)
Lal Kurti, Meerut -- 250 001 (INDIA)
Ph. : Off. (0121) -- 2645252
e-mail : minibooks.publishers@gmail.com

Laser Typesetting :
Sunbeam Computers, Meerut

Printed at :
J.C.T. Offset, Meerut

Preface

This book ***Junior School Essays*** is being introduced with emphasis on this very fact, that one should have a clear comprehension with coherent expression so as to be successful in today's competitive world. Motive behind this venture is to help develop the power of expression and communicative skill of the students.

To educate the people not only for the sake of degree and job but also for knowledge, the new education policy of Government of India lays stress on reducing the load of books and prescribes functional literacy.

This book includes essays on various topics relating to different subjects. To introduce certain novelties in the present book all necessary changes have been incorporated.

This book will sure help the students to a great extent suggestions regarding improvement are welcome.

Author

CONTENTS

ESSAYS

❶ WHAT IS AN ESSAY ?

An essay is, generally speaking, a written composition containing an expression of one's personal opinions or ideas on a subjects. Dr. Johnson defines an essay as "a loose sally of the mind; an irregular, indigested piece, not a regular and orderly composition." According to A. C. Benson, "the essential point about an essay is not the subject but the charm of personality" which pervades the entire essay. The information supplied by the Oxford Concise Dictionary is that an essay is "a literary composition on any subject, usually in prose, and short."

❷ SELECTION OF SUBJECT

Essay may deal with an almost endless variety of subjects. "Anything will serve the essayist, from the death of a great generally or a great author to a chalk-mark on the door." He can choose any subject he likes "from the stars to dust-heaps and from the amoeba to man", or as Lynd puts it, "anything from the Day of judgement to a pair of scissors." Even a pin seen on the road may set him amusing, or he may write an essay on "Nothing".

❸ PARTS OF THE ESSAY

An essay is usually divided into three parts :

(1) The Introduction.

(2) The Body

(3) The Conclusion

(1) The Introduction. The introduction should be brief. It should not be bigger than the body of the essay itself. It generally consists of a very short paragraph. But, it should always be very striking and interesting. It should arrest the attention of the reader and induce him to read on. It should give a definition or explanation of the title. It should strike the keynote on the essay and tell the reader what to expect.

(2) The Body. This is the main part of the essay. It consists of the appropriate facts, anecdotes, figures, illustrations, reflections and quotations. Here you should follow closely your outline. The paragraphs should be well connected. If the topic asked is scientific or historical or geographical, the essay should not bristle with figures and dates and formulae. Only things of general interest should be given.

(3) The Conclusion. The ending, like the beginning, should be short and striking. It should be natural and not forced. It should not be abrupt. It should never give the impression that the writer has been forced to stop due to want of time or space or matter but that he has arrived at his destination and finished writing all he wanted to write on the topic.

❹ STYLE IN WRITING AN ESSAY

The style in which an essay is to be written is the most important. The following points should be paid attention to :

(1) Take great care to make use of only such words and phrases as exactly express the views and ideas that you have in your mind.

(2) Frame your sentences in such a manner that they are short, lucid and intelligible.

(3) Avoid making use of unnecessary words.

(4) Do not employ a word or a phrase the meaning of which you do not know.

(5) Be brief, say what you want to say as briefly as you can. Never use ten words where one will do.

(6) Be natural, do not try to copy others. Express your own ideas in your own manner.

(7) Avoid flowery language. Do not employ bombastic or high-sounding words and phrases.

❺ IMPORTANT HINTS ON ESSAY-WRITING

Keep in mind the following steps :

(1) Never start writing at once. Think out carefully for five or ten minutes what you are going to a remark.

(2) Write down the various ideas that come to your mind.

(3) Select your ideas very attentively. Deal with your ideas very effectively.

(4) Stick to these points. It is useless to write down a lot of things that having nothing to do with the subject.

(5) Arrange your ideas. You cannot create a good essay without a plan. Therefore, you must make a plan and arrange your ideas so systematically that they follow one another naturally.

(6) Divide your essay into paragraphs. Write a fresh para on each point in accordance with the plan.

(7) Divide your essay into three parts, the introduction, the body and the conclusion.

(8) Make use of simple words and short sentences.

(9) Be clear as well as relevant.

(10) Be interesting as well as arresting.

(11) Revise carefully what you have written. Try your almost to remove all the mistakes in spelling, capital letters, grammar, punctuation, etc.

❑❑❑

MYSELF [HE]

My name is Ayush Nanda. I am four years old. I was born at Meerut. I have one brother. His name is Vikas. My father, K. S. Nanda, is a professor. My mother, Kamla, is a teacher. My aunt Shashi is famous social reformer. I have four uncles. My uncle, Deepak is a Army Officer. My grand-father is also a teacher. My great grand-father was a retired Police Inspector. We live at Delhi now. I read in St. Johns school. Everyone in the house likes me. They call me Chinto.

Myself [She]

My name is Nitika Nanda. I am five years old. I was born at Delhi. I have one brother. His name is Jatin. My father, Shri A. K. Nanda, is a Engineer in private limited factory. My mother, Sangeeta, is a housewife. My aunt Rita is famous social reformer. I have two uncles. My uncle, Deepak is a Army Officer. My grandfather is retired from army. My great grand-father was a retired as Army Captain. We are living in Delhi since last six years. I read in Faith Academy school. Everyone in the house likes me. They call me Niti.

MY BIRTHDAY

Tomorow is 24th April. It is my birthday. I am six years old. Tomorrow I shall be seven year old.

I have seen seven springs. And I have seen as many winters. Birthday is a happy event. I have invited by classmates and friends. My Grandfather and Grandmother will also come.

I remember my last birthday. All my friends came on that day. There was a large gathering. They brought many nice presents and birthday wishing cards.

MyGrandmother and Grandfather wished me a long life. My friends wished me many returns of the day. They clapped and sang birthday songs.

They there was a birthday party. We had many sweets like biscuits, sweddish etc. We had soft drinks also. There were many salty dishes.

MY HOBBY

A hobby is an interesting thing. It gives great pleasures. It makes life interesting. It is something done in spare time. It is not done for money. People's hobbies difer very much according to the character of the person himself. What would appeal to one man might be the subject of ridicule to another. The best form of recreation is one that can develop in one awareness, colour, concentration and an observational power. In pursuance of a hobby, one can enjoy one's leisure and learn at the same time.

There are many activities in our life, which can be developed into hobbies or interest. One should choose a hobby wisely. Reading, gardening, indoor games, painting, writing, singing, dancing, reading for a blind boy or even decorating a house etc. are some well known hobbies. Denise Robins, queen of romantic writers, with 145 novels to her name, cultivates roses.

Hobbies fill a gap. It can lift our spirit when we are depressed. It makes us creative. Many friendship are formed among people who have common hobbies. The unique quality of a person can be developed with the help of a good hobby.

It eases your mind to be absorbed in something. You have something to show to your friends and something which is educating and brings relaxation to a tired mind. Many hobbies can be used commercially and it can bring fame. Hobby is constructive. It gives the mind something positive to hold on to. Nothing can make you feel bore while you have an interesting hobby to turn to.

MY MOTHER

My name is Ayush Nanda. My mother's name is Benu Nanda. She was born at Kanpur. Shri Yudhisthir Verma is her father. Her mother name is Shrimati Neelam Verma. She had two sister. All of them are housewifes. Elder sister have two sons. Another one have one son and one daughter. Her father was a Air Force Officer. She has only son. She is housewife. She remained busy in household works. She also help me in teaching. She tells me decent stories of Raja Maharaja and fairy tales. She is 30 years old. She is very active and smart lady.

MY FATHER

My name is Ayush Nanda. Shri Arvind Nanda is my father. He is thirty years old. He is a Computer Engineer in private factory. He is posted at Meerut. He is tall and handsome. He is very hard-working man.

He is sincere in his duties. He teaches me daily and also help me in completing home work. He belongs to the family of business. He is a nice gentleman. He enjoys good health. He has all the good qualities of head and heart. He loves me very much. I am proud of him.

MY BROTHER

Jatin is my brother. He is four years old. He can count upto two hundred. He has learnt ten poems by heart. Varun and Gaurav are our cousins. He is very smart. He plays cricket with me. He is very naughty. He can drive the baby-tricycle.

He is quite healthy. He is fair in colour. He is a promising chap. My parents and uncles like and love him. He has sweet nature. He goes to bed early and leaves the bed early. He never takes tea. He is playful and cheerful. He is the light of our house.

MY SISTER

Nitika is my sister. She is seven years old. She is sixth class. She is very intelligent and sweat nature girl. She lives with us. She is quite healthy. She is very kind and gentle. She helps me in my studying. She used to play badminton with me. She is also a good story-teller. She keeps discipline in her house. She loves me lot. She never tells a lie. She always wants to live in discipline. She always stood first in her class. Her teachers and classmates like her very much.

She respects all elders. Her hobbies is reading fairy tales. She lives in big and spacious house. Her two She always remains cheerful.

MY GRAND MOTHER

My grandmother is a very old lady. Her name is Krishna Nanda. She has already crossed fifty-five. Even at this age, she is very active and hard-working. At times, we are surprised at her agility. She supervises all important jobs in the family. Some she does herself. She is tall and thin. She is grey haired and her humble and affectionate face is full of wrinkles. Her eye-sight, however, is quite good and she read without spectacles.

She is a religious lady. But her devotion to religion and God does not disturb rest of the family. She is the first to leave her bed in the early morning. Before we get up, she has already taken her bath with fresh water. Immediately after bath, she goes to the temple. We eagerly wait for her to come back for she brings Prasad for us.

She is very affectionate and caring. We, her grandchildren are attached to her more than to our parents. She is never cross with us. Her love for us is her passion. But she is equally generous to other children. My father and my uncle always seek her advice in all social matters. She is the most respected lady in our colony. Ladies, young and old, come to her for advice. Sometimes they bring their problems. In the afternoon many women flock around her. They feel flattered in doing her a little service. Sometimes she tells them her own experiences. They listen to her with respect.

Like all old women, she has some orthodox habits but unlike other old women, she has a surprising quality to change with the time. Nobody forces her, but she herself has changed many of her superstitious habits. We all are thankful to God for such a loving grandmother.

MY GRAND FATHER

Shri Kasturi Lal Nanda is my grand father. He lived in Roorkee. He is 72 years old. He is retired army officer. He was a able administrator. He gets pension for 14 years. He kept sound health. He started his day at 4 a.m. He went out for a daily morning walk. When he came here he helps me in study. He used to tell us good fairy stories at night. He was noble and respectable. He is also a social worker. He was held in respect. He had all the good qualities of head and heart.

A LOVELY BABY

Anshul is lovely baby. She is one years old. Mihir is her brother. Her mother is a school teacher. Neena is her sister. Her father is Air Force Officer. She was born at Meerut. She ia very smart. She has two uncles. She has one maternal uncles. She lives with her parents in Meerut. She has pleasing manners. Everyone in the neighourhood likes her.

MY HOME

My name is Varun. I live at 321, Subhash Puri, Meerut. My house is neat and clean. It has seven rooms. It has a big kitchen. It has a bath-room, a store-room and a lavatory. Its floors are cemented. Each room has two doors, two windows and two ventilators.

We have a lovely drawing-room. We have spread a carpet on its floor. I have a separate room. I study in it. My home is the best and the safest place for me. I like my home very much.

MY FAMILY

My family is small. We are four members in all. There are my parents, my brother and I. My brother is elder to me. He is in the sixth grade. My brother and I go to the same school. We go together by school bus. The school is far from our house.

My father is in State Bank of India. His bank is in Mall Road, Meerut. He goes there by own vehicle. When we are all together, we have a lot of fun. My father tells us manyk jokes. His jokes are always fresh and new.

My mother is a house wife. But, she also enjoys fun. She is a religious lady. She is very popular among women. She loves children. She can be often seen with them. She always keep him busy in household works.

My parents are loving and kind. They give us everything we want and deserve.

MY SCHOOL

I read in St. Paul Public School, Lucknow. It has a big building. It has about 55 class rooms. It has two laboratories. It has a large library. The library contains a large number of books, newspapers and magazines. All the rooms in our school are airy and spacious. Our school has a big dispensary.

Our school playground is very big. The students play hockey, cricket, football and volleyball in it. Our school is counted among goods schools in Lucknow. It is on the top in sports and studies. The school staff is highly educated. Our school shows good results every year. Our Principal Sh. R. K. Jain is very able and kind. All teachers take pains in teaching the students. The school has good discipline. There is a rush in the school at the time of admission.

MY PRINCIPAL

I read in a Bhartiya Girls Senior Secondary School. Mrs. Anu Ahuja is the Principal of our school. She is an M.A., B.Ed. She is a great disciplinarian. She guides the teachers and the students. She is regular and punctual in her duty.

She believes in simple living and high thinking. She inspects the classes daily. She addresses the morning assembly daily. She gives great importance to games. She helps the poor students. She gives extra coaching to weak students. She is popular among the staff and the students. She plays the role of a guardian too.

MY FIRST DAY IN SCHOOL

I still remember my first day in school. Then I was five years old. It was an interesting day for me. My mother had waken me up early in the morning. After bath and breakfast, I put on my school uniform. I felt a little excited. My elder brother was in the 3rd grade in the same school.

My father took us there by scooter. We walked into the compound. It was full of boys and girls. We went to the Principal. He admitted me to the first staandard. Then my father left for his office.

I was led to my classroom. The class-teacher was kind. She made me sit in the first row. The students were nice and friendly.

In the recess I went to the tuck shop. My brother was already there. We had our refreshment together. He had brought it from home. At 11.30 a.m. the bell rang, and the school was over. My brother came to bring me. My mother met us at the gate. She came to pick us up in a cab.

MY CLASS TEACHER

My class-teacher is a charming lady. She is stout. She is of fair colour. Her name is Miss Anu Ahuja. She teaches us English and Maths. She is about 35 years of age. She is always cheerful.

She is a nice teacher. She never gets angry when a student fails to learn. She encourages him or her to learn again and again. She explains things in simple and clear manner. She is gentle and soft-spoken.

She is always ready to help her pupils. But she is very strict in discipline. She always wants us to be disciplined and tidy.

I am glad that Miss Anu Ahuja is my class-teacher. She makes her teaching interesting with the help of charts, maps, or toys. Sometimes she takes us on a visit to some

MY NEIGHBOUR

Ram Prasad is my neighbour. He is sixty years old. He has a small family. He is a man of good nature. His wife is a noble lady. He has one daughter and one son. He makes all types of wooden furniture. He repairs our chairs, stools and tables. He is very simple in his dress.

He is very hard-working. He is very helpful to all his neighbours. He never gets angry with anyone. All the neighbours like him. We have homely relations with him. He is sincere in his work. I like him very much.

MY BEST FRIEND

Suresh Wadhwa is my best friend. He is of my age. He lives at Meerut. He is my class-fellow. He is the moniter of my class. His father is a shop-keeper. His mother is pious lady. He has one brother and one sister.

He stands first in the class every year. He is very obedient to the teachers. He is very hard-working. He is very helpful to his chass-mates. He is quite simple in dress and habits. He never tells a lie. He never makes false promises. He helps his parents at home. He is in the good books of the teachers. I am proud of him. I love him dearly.

MY SERVANT

Ramu is our servant. He is an old man of fifty. He is a poor man. He is undergraduate. He makes tea for our family. He cleans and dusts our house every day. He also washes our clothes. We pay him Rs 1000/- per month. He also get s food and clothing.

He is hard-working. Sometimes he steals money from my purse. His children do not serve him. He cheats us whenever we ask him to make any purchases. He falls on our feet when we scold him. He has no one to support him. He would be forced to become a beggar if we turn him out of job. He back-bites everbody. Though he is mean, yet we have to take pity on him.

OUR SCHOOL PEON

One who sits outside the Principal's office is called a school peon. He is an important person. Principal knows that school cannot do without him.

Ram Naresh is our school peon. He is about fifty years. He is a tall man. He possesses strong body. He is quite healthy. He has wheatist complexion. He belongs to a small village.

He is all the time in khaki uniform. He wears a white Gandhi cap. He gets uniform every year from the school. He lives in a small room in the school compound. He is a married person. His wife and children live in the village.

He has one hundred and one duties to do. He comes an hour before the opening of the school. He cleans the Principal's room. He dusts desks, tables and chairs in the class rooms. He then rings the bell.

As long as the school goes on, he sits near the Principal's office. He carries out his orders. Sometimes he goes to post letters. Sometimes he has to go to the bank to deposit or withdraw school money. Sometimes he circulates an order in the classes. At other times he shows the visitors in. He does all this and other duties also. He goes on ringing the bell at the end of each period. Sometimes, if he is irregular in his duties, everybody complains against him, because the school work begins to suffer.

When it is time to close the school, he rings the close bell. He shuts all the doors and windows after the boys have gone. He then puts the keys in his pocket and goes home.

He lives a hard life. He gets a small salary of five hundred rupees in a month. With the small income he cannot keep his family with him. In the town he cannot support his family. He has been in the service of this school for the last thirty years.

OUR SCHOOL SWEEPER

There are four sweeper in our school. Ramu is one of them. He belongs to a village. He is fifty years old. He keeps a broom with a long handle. He brooms the Principal's office, the staff-room, the school office, the library and the laboratories. He is hard-working and dutiful. He is honest and strong.

He lives in the school campus. His pay is very small. He has a large family. So life is very hard for him. The principal should show kindness to him.

THE COW

The cow is the most useful animal to mankind. Hindus regard her sacred like their mother and worship her.

The cow is a quadruped bovine animal with a big body and long tail. The tail ends with a tuft of hairs which is used for driving away flies and mosquitoes. She has two big sharp horns on the head along with two long ears and two blue shining eyes. She has sharp teeth in its jaws for eating vegetarian food. She has split hooves under its four legs. These hooves allow her to walk through a mud and soil. An extra hanging skin under the neck is a significant feature found in the cow and ox.

The cows are distributed all over the globe and are tamed by the people throughout the world. The European and American cows are stronger and bigger in size than the Indian ones. They are found in various colours. They are generally white, black, brown and of yellowish and reddish tints. Certain cows are of mixed colours. Some cows are found with different coloured spots all over their body. They are of five to six feet lengthwise from head to tail and four to five feet heightwise.

Cow is a tame domestic animal which is liked by all of us. She is ruminating animal. She eats the food fast and chews the cud while at rest to digest it. Young children feel very glad to play with cows and calves. The calves are jovial and jubiliant active and beautiful to look at and play with. The cow eats grass, straw, hay, oil-cake, cotton seeds, rice-bran, pulse peels and vegetables etc. She eats fodder which is purely vegetarian and simple but she gives plenty of nutritious and delicious milk. Cow's milk is almost a full food for young and aged alike. It is a wholesome diet for the sick and children. Curd, butter, ghee, cheese and sweets made from cow's milk are not only tasty but are healthy for the body and mind.

The cow is a very faithful animal to her master. Though it appears strange a few incidents relating to the bravery of bovinal animals in saving their master, from ferocious carnivorous creatures are known.

Beyond cow's milk the dung is also used for plastering the floors and walls of the rural houses even today as it kills harmful germs. Dung cakes are used as cooking fuel in villages. Now a days gobar gas plants are installed which consume lots of dung and provide cooking gas and we get manure to the fields. According to the Hindu faith the combination of cows milk, curd, urine and dung mixture is both pious and efficacious in the rituals.

Even after death cow's hide is useful to make leather articles like shoes, belts, bags and boxes etc. Her bones and horns are used for making useful articles like combs, phosphorus etc.

In our country cow-slaughter is not prohibited by the law. Even though many of us want the prohibition of cow-slaughter, yet none of us give reasonable solution to the dangerous question of providing food and shelter to the old and forlorn cows. When this problem is solved a prdeable banning of cow-laughter may become a reality. Let us, hope that we may repay our debt to our "Mother-cow" by protecting her from the agony of cruel killing not only sentimentally but by the law as well !

THE CAT

It is a cat. It is my pet animal. It is found in the all parts of the world. It has four legs. It has a tail.

It has two ears. It has two shining eyes. It has sharp teeth. Its legs are thin. It eats bread. It drinks milk. The mouse is its favorite prey. It is found in many colours. It can run very fast. It has a keen sense of smell. It keeps mewing every time. It has sharp nails. Young children play with the kittens. It is a terror to the rats.

THE DOG

The dog is a pet animal. They make us feel family member. The dogs are pet animals which are most faithful to man. There are several facts associated with their bravery faithfulness and cleverness. The dog is a quadruped and a carnivorous animal.

Dogs are of many colours. Usually they are of brown, black, white and red colours. Yet some are found with mixed, spotted or patched colours on their skin. The fur-dogs have coat with full of hairs, Generally they have coat of short thick hairs but few are found with no hair on their skin. They have sharp teeth and rough tongue to eat meat as it is a carnivorus. They have tufty short and long tails with long droopy or straight ears. The dog has soft pads of flesh under his paws. The height and size of dog differs very much. Some are very tiny and certain very huge and massive in their built. Mostly they are of two to three feet of height and length.

The dog can be trained to show obedience and it is the best friend of man. He is an affectionate companion who finds way into the personal life of man. He attacks on command and guards the property. He serves his master faithfully; sometimes at the cost of his life even. He is never found idle but always alert and keeps night vigil. He is used by military and para military forces for finding nout explosive and other illicit things. He is employed by police for detective work, to find out stolen and smuggled good, narcotics, thieves, murderers and criminals. Bombay police force dog-squad did wonders in this respect.

Dog when they become mad they are to be feared as their bite may be fatal. One should be very careful about mad dogs, when such a dog bites, a doctor should be consulted soon for proper medical care.

THE ANT

The ant is generally found in every house. They are tiny creatures and bite very sharply. They are found in open fields and closed abodes. According to climate and season their number increases and decreases. They come out of thier nests in great numbers in humid climate. The ant is a tiny insect. The head of it has two eyes, a pair of antennae and biting mouth parts. Its body has three parts which are connected with each other by a thin fibre.

They are different sizes and kinds of ants. Some are very tiny and some are big. There are red ants and black ants found everywhere in the houses crawling on food articles etc. The black ants do not bite but the red ones bite sharply. There are big size black ants also which are found creeping on trees, farms, fields and in homes. These ants when bite produce severe pain and some time even blood also comes out. There are white ants which are called as termites. They destroy books, clothes, wood, timber and furniture.

The ants eat flour, sugar, gur, sweets and dead products. The ant has an acute sense of smell and finds the odour of its food from a long distance. Even if, one ant comes to know of food the other ants receive message and com ein great numbers to swap the food. They carry food particles in their mouth and proceed to their nests in a row. They gather food all through summer and store it for winter season. The ants keep and tend ant-cow for its honey-dew. The ant-cow is a certain kind of green fly which collects nectar of flowers. The name of ant is synonymous with labour and industry. They do not take rest and they work very hard. Ants are good builders. They build their nests which are called ant hills. The ant hills when deserted by ants are used by snakes. These ant hills are divided into different compartments. They construct their nests unitedly and harmoniously for communal living. Communal harmony, industry, labour and co-operative way of living should be learnt by man from the ants and their living.

The ants though menace to us as they swap our food-stuffs but they are also useful to us. They sweep away dead insects and other dirty things. They white ants render useful-service to man by consuming dead wood and vegetation. They aid in agriculture by enriching the soil and by making the soil permeable to air and moisture.

The ant-bear is the enemy of ants. It eats ants in large numbers with extreme fascination.

THE HONEY BEE

The honey bee is a social insect. It is a fly know to man for its usefulness from olden times. The bees are found mostly in tropical countries. Throughout India we find rock bee, the Indian little bee and the Indian bee which are longer, smaller and medium ones respectively. Bees are also found in North-Africa, Europe and in Southern Russia as well.

Honey bees are mostly vegetable feeders. Adults chiefly live upon honey while the young ones are fed with pure pollen or pollen mixed with honey and water. Bees thrive best in the forests and gardens. They live in hives. Bee-hives are made by the wax produced by them. In a hive there are several parallel combs which are divided into hexagonal shaped cells. The cells are divided for storing honey, for living and for laying eggs etc. Bees construct their hives in protective places like under caves of buildings or the hollow of trees or on the branches. In these hives several thousands of bees live together in a highly organised and disciplined way. They are industrious, laborious and extremely busy. They live harmoniously and work for the common good of the colony.

In a colony there are three types of bees namely queen or fertile female, drones or males and workers or sterile females. The queen bee's function is, to lay eggs and increase the number of bees. The male bees do not work in any kind except mating with the queen. The number of worker bees is very much greater than the queen and the male bees. They attend all duties of food collection like bringing nectar from the flowers, they tend the young and serve the male and queen bees. They produce wax to build the hives skilfully. They protect the queen and the hive from enemies.

The colour of the bee is usually brown or black. It has small body with tiny head. The head contains a pair of eyes, two antennae, a trunk to suck nectar and a stinge to bite the enemy. It has two tiny legs in the front and four sturdy legs in the middle and hind parts. It has two wings. There are bees like flying and humming ones other than honey bee also.

The honey-bees move in s warms and make several thousand trips to bring honey from distant places to the hive. They collect the nectar from each and every flower by sucking it with their trunk.

Honey bees are very useful to man; they provide honey, bees-wax and also help us pollinators. Without bees fruit formation in orchards and grooves will reduce very much. Thus bees help very much indirectly for our agriculture economy.

Bee keeping is a very good and useful to pass time that improves the economy of man. Birds and wasps are the enemies of the bees. Man, it seems to be the worst enemy of the bees.

THE HORSE

The horse is a graceful animal. It is also a noble animal and very useful for man. A horse is known for its beauty and strength. It has been the companion of man from ancient days. It can run a long distance. It is a very useful animal. It is used for riding, racing pulling carts and cultivating lands. In olden times it was used for fighting a battle. It is clever and can learn many tricks. It serves its master faithfully. It can dance and jump. Many tales tell how it served its master courageously. Circus horse perform wonderful feats. The horse is a part of American Cow-boy's life. It is said Napoleon slept on horse-back.

Man's love for the horse is well-known. The Arabian horses are famous. The horses live mainly on grass. It also likes grams. A Male horse is called `stallion', the female `mare'. A male baby horse is called a colt. A female baby horse is called a foal.

The horses neigh. it was originally a wild animal. But many domesticated it. In grace there are not many animals to match a horse.

THE CAMEL

The camel is a pet animal. It has a large body. It has a very long neck. It has a hump on its back. It has thin legs. It has sharp and long teeth. It has a small tail, two eyes and two ears. It is a very strong animal. It fills its stomach with water. It can live for many days without taking water. Its colour is grey. It eats grass, leaves, sugarcane, shrubs and bushes. It is generally nine to ten feet high. It can carry heavy loads through the desert. It is found in hot countries. It is called the 'ship of the desert'. It is used for riding fast on the sand. It gives out a grunting sound.

THE ELEPHANT

Most of us have seen many kinds of animals. The elephant is one of the most impressive animals found in India. We have seen it either on the street or in some zoo. Most of us have great love and respect for this big animal.

The elephant is a very big animal from eight to ten feet tall. It has a dark grey coloured skin, four huge pillar-like legs, a long nose or spout and usually two long ivory teeth. It has two small eyes. It has fan-like ears. It has a short tail. It is a very strong but gentle animal. It is fond of muddy water. It has a long trunk. It has two white tusks. Elephant are trained to do heavy work. They were used in battle fields in old time. It can carry heavy loads. It is also used for riding. A leather saddle is put on its back. It walks slowly. It can swim in the water. It can run fast on land. The elephants love to eat sugarcanes. It becomes fearful when it gets must. It is a costly and useful animal. It is the largest and strongest animal.

It is definitely a very useful animal. It can be used as a means of transport. Besides, because of its great strength, it can carry heavy weights, such as logs of woods. In addition, it is also a very intelligent animal, with a powerful memory. People say that an elephant never forgets anyone who has over done it some kindness or caused it some harm. It never harms a person without any reason. Thirdly, an elephant is also a peaceful and friendly animal. We often see children playing around it, when some sadhu brings an elephant into our town.

In the end, we can say that the elephant is a very fine animal. Inspite of its great strength, it is kind and gentle.

THE LION

The lion is a wild animal. It is a beast of prey. It is a very strong and brave animal. Lions are mostly found in thick forests. They are generally reddish-brown or golden in colour. The lion has strong jaws and paws. It has a thick mane of hair on its shoulders and head. It ia a fearless animal. It gives out a loud roar. It kills its prey with a single blow of its paw. It tears its prey into small pieces. The lion is called the king of the jungle. Flesh is its favourite diet. The other beasts are afraid of the lion.

THE CROW

The crow is found every where. It flies in the sky on its wings. The crow is jet black in colour. It has two sharp eyes. It has two claws. It has a long and pointed beak. It eats meat; worms and bread. It snatches pieces of bread from small children. It can fly high in the air. It makes its nest on trees and lives there. It is a bold and clever thief.

It caws all the time. No one likes to keep the crow as a pet. When it caws it means some guest is about to come. It is a cunning bird. It preys on small birds. It clears away dirty things.

A PEACOCK

The peacock is India's national bird. A peacock is a very beautiful colour bird. It is a found in many parts of India. When a peacock dances, it spread out its feathers like a fan. Its feathers are multi-coloured. It has long and lovely feathers. Its feathers are used to make many beautiful things. The peacock is a dancing bird.

A peacock has a long shining, dark, blue neck. Its call is loud and sweet. It can fly only over very short distances. . It dances during rains. It has a crown (crest) on its head. It can open its tail like a great fan. It also has a crown on its head. The female peacok is called a peahen. The peahen has no feathers. It is a bulky bird. It cannot fly very high. It lives on trees. It is fond of chillies. It has an acute sense of hearing. It is a harmless bird.

A peacock is a great friend of farmers. It eats up harmful insects. Thus, it protects crops and plants. Peacock dance is a popular dance. In it the dance movements of the bird are imitated. A peacock dance done in a group is a fascinating sight.

Its legs are ugly. It sheds tears when it looks at its feet while dancing.

A CHAIR

It is a chair. It is made of wood. It has four legs. It has a back. It has two arms. A carpenter made it. Its seats is made of cane. Its colour is brown. It is polished. I keep it against the table. I sit in it and study. It is a beautiful chair. It cost is two hundred rupees. I have bought it from Sadar Bazaar. I like it very much. I feel pleasure in sitting in it. It is wide and comfortable.

A TABLE

It is a table. It is made of teak wood. It has four legs. Its colour is brown. A carpenter made it. It is three feet long and two feet wide. It is polished. It is two and half feet high. It has no drawer. My father bought it from Sadar Bazaar. Its price is three hundred rupees. I keep the table in my room. I dust it daily. I keep my chair by its side. I place my books and exercise books on it. It is very useful to me. It keeps me active. I take my tea on it. I like it much.

THE BLACK-BOARD

It is a black-board. It is black in colour. It is made of wood. It is kept on a wooden-stand. It is in our class-room. A carpenter made it. The principal bought it from Begum-bridge market. Our teahers write on it with a piece of chalk. Its price is four hundred rupees. It is very useful. The teachers write important matter (points) on it. It helps the students in understanding. The students copy down from the black-board in the exercise-books. We clean it with a duster.

OUR CLASS TEACHER

A teacher is highly respected in India. He or she deserves this respect as a builder of the nation. There are, however, various categories of teachers. Some are respected, some are feared. Some of the teachers are highly in telligent, some are only mediocre. There are others who may be intelligent but cannot make the students understand. Only a teacher with the qualities of head and heart and ability to make students understand is respected.

Mrs Payal Abrol is our class teacher. She is thirty years old. She is punctual in her work. She is She lives at Meerut. She is an M.A.; M.Ed. She is quite able and intelligent. She teaches us English. She teaches eighth and ninth classes. She is very kind and smart. She has good character. She was a student in this school too. She always keeps in touch with the latest methods of teaching. She reads the relevent magazines and books. She is a past master in the art of understanding student psychology.

She has a special qualification. She has studied linguistics. So, she teaches us correct pronunciation of English words. She is very particular about grammer also. She takes real pains. She corrects the exercise-books of all the students. Though a laborious job, she does it pleasantly. She explains everything so nicely. She brings everything home to the students.

She encourages students to ask unhesitantly what they do not follow. She comes down to the level of the students. Whole of the class is satisfied with her teaching. There is thus no noise in the class.

In addition, she is herself a great orator. She has won many prizes in declamation contests during her college days. So, she has taken upon herself the duty of preparing the students for declamation, debates and other activities. It is all due to her efforts that our school students got first prize in a declamation context held at the Arya School only recently.

More than a teacher, she is our friend, philosopher and guide. SShe treats the students as her own children. She never beats or schools us. She helps the poor boys with money and clothes. All the members of the staff respect her. She is in the good books of the principal. She belongs to a respectable family. I am proud of her.

A PEN

It is a pen. It is my pen. It is black in colour. It is round in shape. Its nib is made of brass. It is made of plastic. Its tube is made of rubber. I clean it daily. Then I fill it with ink. It writes smoothly.

It is like a friend to me. I always keep my pen with me. I write with my pen on the paper. I bought it for eight rupees. I like it very much.

A PENCIL

It is a pencil. It is my pencil. It is round in shape. It is green in colour. It is made of wood and lead. Its lead is black. Its wood is hard and lead is soft.

It is used to write with. It is very lovely. I always keep it with me. I do not lend it to anyone. Its cost is one rupee only. I draw pictures with it everyday. Its trade mark is 'Kohinoor'. It is about seven inches long. It helps me much like a friend. I like it very much.

A KNIFE

It is a knife. It is used for cutting things. We can cut fruit, vegetables and many other things with it. We can also mend the pencil with it. It has two parts. Its handle is made of wood. Its blade is made ot steel or iron. Its blade is very sharp. The handle is blunt. Its price is five rupees. I bought it from Chandni Chowk. It is shining knife.

A BOOK

It is a book. It is a book of Composition and Grammer. It is made of paper. It has a lovely cover.

It has 190 pages. It contains many coloured pictures. I learn spellings and rules of grammer from it.

It is a very useful book. Its price is ten rupees. I bought it from Old Sarak, Meerut. Pankaj Bist wrote it. It is to read and learn. I like this book very much. It is my true guide. Its language is very simple. I am proud of having such a nice book.

THE POSTMAN

The postman is a public servant. He wears a khaki uniform. He carries a leather bag. He delivers letters, parcels and money orders. He goes from door to door. His work is very hard. His pay is very small. He gets many gifts during festivals. He is very honest an punctual. He brings sad and good news from our relatives and friends. He lives from hand to mouth. He deserves our sympathy.

THE POLICEMAN

The policeman is a public servant. He wears a khaki uniform and a red turban. He keeps law and order. At night he does the work of a watchman. He catches the thieves and the law-breakers. He is healthy, tall and smart.

He performs his duties actively and regularly. He is not highly educated. His life is very hard.

His income is very low. He lives from hand to mouth. The government should increase his pay.

DELHI

This is Delhi. It is quite a big city. It has two parts Old Delhi and New Delhi. It is situated in the bank of river Yamuna. Qutab Minar and the Red Fort are famous buildings in Delhi. Karol Bagh, Chandni Chowk and Connaught Place are its famous bazaars. Raj Ghat, Shanti Vana, Vijay Ghat and Gandhi Sadan are tourist spots in Delhi. There are many big hospitals in Delhi. It is the capital of India. There are many colonies in and Delhi. Bus services are cheap in Delhi. There are many universities in Delhi. Delhi is the dil (heart) of India.

MY COUNTRY

I am privileged to be the son of Mother India. I am her son as I live on the produce of her fields. India is a vast country. She lies in the South of Asia. She is the land of ninty nine crore people. The Himalayas are on her north. The Indian ocean is to her south.

She is the mother of Rama, Krishna, Mahavira, Gautam, Guru Nanak, Daynand and Vivekanand etc. She has given birth to warriors like Porus, Rana Pratap, SHivaji and Rani Jhansi etc. She has given birth to great men like Mahatma Gandhi and Jawaharlal Nehru. She has given birth to freedom fighters like Bhagat Singh, Lala Lajpat Rai and Subhash Chandra Bose. She has given birth to administrators like Sardar Patel. There are hundreds and thousands more that need mention.

India's soil is very fertile. Many crops grow here. She has many industries, mines and forests. Her people speak different languages. They follow different religions. The Ganga is her holy river.

India is rich but Indians are poor. I am proud of my country. I shall live, suffer and die for her sake.

THE MANGO

It is a mango. It is a nice fruit. Its taste is sweet. It is called the king of fruits. It grows on tall trees in the gardens. The skin, the pulp and the stone are its various parts. Its stone and skin are thrown away. Its pulp and juice are as sweet as sherbet.

There are many kinds of mangoes in India. All mangoes are not alike in taste, size and colour. Mangoes are also useful in making jams and pickles. It is very useful for health. Its seed is inside that stone.

AN APPLE

It is an apple. Its taste is sweet. It is very useful for health. It has a skin. We may or may not peel the skin to eat it. Everybody cannot buy this costly fruit.

Apples are found in the hills. They differ in taste, size and colour. Apples are useful in making juice and jam. The apples of Kashmir and Kullu are very famous and tasty.

THE MOON

This is the moon. We see her in the sky. She shines at night. She gives light to the earth. Her light is brighter than the light of stars. It is pleasing to look at the bright moon. The moon does not shine every night. Moon light is cool. The moon changes its size and shape every night. The moon is the Queen of night. The moon goes round the earth. She gets light from the sun. Everyone likes the moonlight in night.

THE SUN

It is the sun. It is a heavenly body. It is like a big ball of fire. It rises in the east every morning. It gives light to the earth. It also gives heat. Its light is dazzling. We cannot look at the sun with naked eyes at noon. The earth revolves round the sun. The sun is the source of light, heat and life. It helps the plants and crops to grow. It sets in the west every evening. it gives light to the moon.

MY AEROPLANE JOURNEY

Last month I experienced my first aeroplane journey from Delhi to Calcutta. I went with my mother. On Thursday morning, we reached the airport on time. At the airport we went through the baggage and security check. Then we got our boardinng passes. Our's was an Indian Airlines Plane. It was very big with many windows. Inside the aeroplane an air-hostess guided us to our seats. My seat was next to the window.

Soon the aeroplane was full. Then the air-hostess exlained how to tie the seat belt and how to use the oxygen mask in case of emergency. The aeroplane took-off. I looked outside my window. Everything on the ground became smaller and smaller.

Inside, the air-hostess served us with cold drinks, toffees and biscuits. The people sitting in the nearby seats were busy talking or reading. One of them was a little boy of my age. We became friends.

The plane landed at Udaipur at 11.20 a.m. It was a short journey but I enjoyed it very much.

MAHATMA GANDHI

Mohandas Karamchand Gandhi was born at Porbandar in Gujarat on 2nd October, 1869. His father was the Diwan of Rajkot. He got higher education in England. He returned India as a lawyer. In South Africa, he fought for the rights of the Indian people.

He worked for Hindu-Muslim unity. He also worked to remove poverty and untouchability. He took part in freedom movement. He went to jail many times. India got freedom under his leadership from British rulers. Truth and Ahimsa were his two great weapons. He was shot dead on 30th January, 1948. He is called the 'Father of the Nation'.

PT. JAWAHAR LAL NEHRU

Pt. Jawahar Lal Nehru was born at Allahabad on November 14, 1889. He got his early education at home. He was sent to England to study law. He returned to India. He came under the influence of Gnadhi. He gave up law. He joined the Indian National Congress.

He fought hard for India's freedom. He went to jail many times. he became the first Prime Minister of free India. He was a great lover of peace. He also believed in the service of humanity. India made all-round progress under his leadership. He died on 27th May, 1964.

A BUS ACCIDENT

Accidents are quite common in big cities like Delhi. Rash and careless driving is the cause of many accidents.

Last Sunday, I saw an accident on Meerut High Way Road. A bus was plying at a fast speed. There was thin traffic on the road. A large number of fast moving vans were visible on the road. A Maruti car was coming at full speed from the opposite side. A small boy was crossing the road. The bus driver ran into the Maruti Car while he was trying to save the boy.

Both the drivers were badly injured. A few passengers of the bus also got light injuries. The police was informed. The injured were removed to the hospital. The driver of the Maruti car died the next day. It was a heavy loss to his family. We should be careful while crossing the busy roads.

A RAILWAY ACCIDENT

Indian Railways are on of the biggest railways running a large number of trains on its tracks. To run the trains on the track properly day and night thousands of railway employees work round the clock vigilantly. Even then certain human error or for unknown reason accidents occur resulting in the loss human lives and crores of property.

One dangerous and unforgettable accident took place on 26th January 1999 near Meerut Cantt Station. When people were sleeping comfortably in the sleeping coaches at small hours of that fateful day a loud voice make up many. Several bogies fell from the railway track. Hundreds of persons who were sitting in the compartments thrown out to the opposite sides; suit cases and other luggage fell on them injuring many. It was pandemonium with wallings, shoutings and cries, everything was confusing. Lights were off to add to the confusion, some passengers who came out of the compartment were giddy and confused. They found to their dismay a terrible scene of head on collision between Southern express and a goods train.

The engine of the Southern express rammed into the engine of goods train. The three front bogies of the express had run into one another and were all smashed. Most of the passengers in those carriages were either killed on the spot or seriously wounded. Those who came out of the other compartments were aghast to witness such a pathetic scene. Blood, was sprawling in the compartments, dead bodies drenched in blood, multiliated bodies, limbs crushed, and cut off spread in all directions. Such a ghastly sight not only shocked but was sickening and nauseating even to see. Wail of cries penetrating the winter mist was miserable and pitiable.

In such a thick fog of early down hours the signaller allowed both the trains on the same railway track. The visibility was poor and the drivers of both the trains blundered as well. The result of these mistakes was the drastic and fateful collision.

Such a head on railway collision due to human error should be avoided in future by being alert and duty conscious. The railway authorities should take proper care so that such accidents which landed in severe loss of men and material may not occur in future.

DROWNING ACCIDENT

It was the Baisakhi day. It is considered auspicious to take bath in flowing water. We decided to go to the Sutlej at Phillaur for a bath. We reached the banks of the Sutlej at 11 a.m.

We were not alone. Hundreds of people of all ages had gathered there. The weather was relaxing. Everyone liked to have a bath. The aged and the children were both near the bank. The water was very shallow there. However, some of the young boys were swimming in the mid stream. The water was very deep there. Currents of water flowed up and down. But they appeared to be enjoying themselves.

Suddenly, a boy was caught in the currents. He began to cry for help. His companions got frightened. They began to withdraw from the scene. However, a dare-devil jumped into the waves. He brought him out with great difficulty.

He was unconscious. His condition was critical. One of the persons knew first-aid. He came running at the scene. He laid the boy on the bank with his face downwards. He applied pressure on his back. A great quantity of water gushed out of his belly. He gave him artificial respiration also. But, he could not succeed.

A few gentlemen hired a taxi and took him to a nearby hospital. But, all these efforts bore no fruit. He was declared dead in the hospital. His parents also reached the hospital. I could not see the crying relatives.

I felt sorry that happy occasions sometimes turn into grief.

A HOUSE ON FIRE

It was midnight. I was enjoying sound sleep. I heard my neighbour crying 'Fire! Fire!'. I reached the scene of fire. I saw a huge crowd. One of the houses in our street was on fire. The smoke was touching the sky.

I saw women running with buckets full of water. I also joined them. We threw water on the fire. The fire spread. It was a terrible sight. A small baby was left inside the house. I took courage. I entered the burning house and brought the child safe.

The fire brigade fought the flames bravely. They brought the fire under control. The whole property was reduced to ashes. Thank God, there was no loss of life.

AN INDIAN FARMER

India is an agricultural country. An Indian farmer is an important person. He grows fruits, corn and vegetables. He grows cotton also. he works hard from morning till evening. He feeds others but himself remains ill-fed.

The farmer ploughs his land. Then he sows the seeds. He waters his fields and removes the weeds. He reaps the crops when the corn ripens. He lives in mud houses. His food is very simple. He never sits idle. The crops are his life and blood. He lives from hand to mouth. He is illiterate. He is satisfied with his life.

THE STREET HAWKER

Street hawkers are a common sight in villages. They move about in streets. They sell eatables and other things of daily use.

Madhu is our street hawker. He sells eatables to the children and women. He shouts his wares in a singing tone. The children buy biscuits, cakes, toffees and groundnut patties from him. He never gives short measures. He keeps the eatables covered with piece of cloth. He comes to our street both at noon and at sunset. He is popular among women and children. He never cheats them. Sometimes he sells his wares on credit. He is very careful about the quality of his eatables. He knows the names of his regular customers. He is an old person but he is very smart. He wears dirty clothes. He lives from hand to mouth.

A BUS JOURNEY

One day, my father decided to show me the historical places in Jodhpur. We purchased five rupee tickets. It was Sunday. The number of buses on the roads was very short. The private buses do not allow the pass holders to travel in them. We got the bus after an hour.

It was fully packed. Many passengers were standing on the foot-board. The bus started. An old man called out that somebody had picked his pocket. The pick-pocket had already got down the running but. A woman cried in vain that her necklace was missing. After covering half the distance, the driver declared that the bus was out of order. On getting down the bus, I found my purse containing cash and the tickets missing. Being helpless, we returned home at noon.

A RAILWAY JOURNEY

Last Sunday, our class teacher took us to Agra to see the Taj Mahal. We reached the railway station and bought the tickets. The train was already standing on the platform. We got into a compartment. The guard blew the whistle. The train moved slowly. Soon the train was out of the city. A cool wind was blowing. The fields, trees and pillars looked moving back fast.

We saw the farmers working in green fields. We kept standing at the entrance because the compartment was fully packed. The passengers were perspiring. Some people were quarrelling for seats. We saw many towns, villages, rivers and canals on the way. We also saw the fruitladen trees. The cattles were grazing on the green grass. The scenery out-side the train was very beautiful. We reached Agra and saw the Taj in moonlight.

THE TAJ MAHAL

The Taj Mahal is situated at Agra on the bank of river Yamuna. It is an historical building. It is made of white marble. Emperor Shah Jahan had made it in memory of his wife, Mumtaz Mahal.

The Taj Mahal is called the wonder of the world. Its construction was completed in twenty years. The Taj looks more beautiful in moon-lights. Thousands of visitors come to see the Taj every day. The tombs of the emperor and the queen are under the dome in a dark chamber. Many couplets from the Quran are written on the walls. Every visitor praises the art and beauty of the Taj.

THE QUTAB MINAR

Delhi has seen many ups and downs. It has been the capital of many kings and emperors. Many historical buildings had been constructed in Delhi by Muslim rulers.

The Qutab Minar is an old historical building. It is the hightest tower in India. It was completed by Qutubuddin Aibak in 12th century. It is situated near Mehrauli. It had seven storeys. Now it has 378 steps to climb up five storeys. One can see the view of Delhi from the top storey. The visitors are allowed to climb-up only one storey. Thousands of visitors come to see it from far and wide. They praise its height and artistic skill. The foreigners also praise the iron pillar near Qutab Minar. Its sight attracts the people.

THE HAPPIEST DAY OF MY LIFE

Life is full of incidents. Some incidents make us happy while others make us sad. My brother was out of job for a number of months. All the members of our family were worried. They were anxious about his career.

We were sippin tea. Just then we received a letter. It was an appointment letter. My brother was offered the job of an accountant in the office of the A.G.C.R.. A wave of joy spread in the family. Just then, we heard the telephone bell ring. It was a message that my elder sister had given birth to a son. Our joy knew no bounds. We arranged a tea party. We invited all of our neighbours. They shared our joy. They also congratulated our brother. It was really the happiest day of my life.

THE SADDEST DAY OF MY LIFE

Life is full of incidents. Some incidents make us happy while others make us sad. 25th December,

1990 was the the saddest day of my life. I got up at 6 o'clock as usual. My mother prepared the breakfast. I took my bath. Breakfast was served to me. As soon as I took the cup of tea, I heard a knock at the door. I opened the door and saw my younger brother. He broke the sad news that my elder brother living in the village, had died at night. I placed the cup of tea on the table. All the members of the family reached the village. We cremated the dead body of our brother, Roshan Lal. At 4 o'clock in the afternoon, we returned to our house at Sarojini Nagar. Just then, I received a telephonic message that my brother-in-law had met with a serious accident. We went to see him in the hospital. He unconscious. I had stay with him all night. Wasn't it the saddest day of our life ?

A VISIT TO ZOO

Zoo is a place where different kinds of birds and animals are kept for show. Last Sunday, I went to see the zoo with a few friends. We bought the tickets and entered the gate. We saw many ducks, cranes and herons in a pond. They were swimming and diving merrily.

Then I saw the stags and deer running here and there. The rhinos looked very fearful. We saw some parrots, pigeons, hawks, owls and sparrow. The small birds looked pretty in the cages. They were chirping in different kinds of notes. We offered grams and ground nuts to the black monkeys and apes. Then we enjoyed the elephant-ride.

In the end, we saw lions, tigers and bears pacing up and down in the sunshine.

The memory of the visit to zoo is still green in my mind. It has added a lot to my knowledge.

A VISIT TO A CICUS-SHOW

A circus is a place of public show. Men, women, wild animals and children show their feats there.

One evening, I went to see the Gemini Circus with a few friends. It was held at Raja Garden. We bought tickets and entered the gate. There were chairs for the spectators. We got our seat. We saw many clowns sitting in the arena.

Just then. the bell rang and the show started. A few young boys and girls showed their feats of gymnastics. Then we saw a group of girls cycling on a wire fixed on two poles. The elephants and lions showed their feats. The feats of dogs, goats and hippoptamus appealed everybody. A man drove a motor-cycle with full speed in the well of death. Last of all we saw a few jokers riding an old motor car. Its parts got separated and the engine seemed to catch fire. The fire-brigade party sprinkled water on the jokers. The memory of my visit to the circus show is still green in my mind.

A VISIT TO A VILLAGE FAIR

Fairs are a part and parcel of rural life. India is a land of villages. More than eighty percent of the people live in the villages. It is, therefore, a fact to say that Indian lives in villages. But, it is strange that most of us have never visited a village. I had long desired to see a village. An opportunity was offered by the Basant fair in a nearby village. Some of my friends readily agreed to accompany me.

Thousands of people had gathered at the fair site. Many more were coming on foot, in bullock carts and in groups. They were coming from the neighbouring villages. All of them were in colourful clothes. Some of the men had turbans on their head. The women were in Salwar Kameez or Sari They were laiden with heavy silver ornaments. Some of them were singing in chorus. They were really in a festive mood.

A kind of temporary bazaar had appeared. On its either side there were booths and stalls. People were making all sorts of purchases. There was a rush of children on toy stalls. Women folk crowded the bangle stalls. There were bangles of beautiful shades and designs. The sweet shops had roaring business.

At a side, there were merry-go-rounds. The children enjoyed the joy-ride very much. The snake-charmers and jugglers attracted large crowds. The rope dancers and magicians were also entertaining the people with their tricks.

In the nearby fields, some persons were flying kites. The kite sellers had a good business. The whole sky was covered with kites of different shades and sizes. It roused a great excitement and uproar in the spectators. Whenever a kite was cut, shouts of `bo-kata' were raised.

In a field, wrestling matches were going on. Wrestlers of different villages made a show of their tricks and might. They were wrestling to the beating of a drum.

Some voluntary organisations had made arrangements for drinking water. Police force was also posted. The policemen kept a watchful eye on bad characters.

It was getting dark. We hired a tonga and came back. We were completely tired but happy. We had a chance to see a village fair and its people.

A VISIT TO THE RED FORT

The history club of our school decided to pay a visit to the Red Fort. We went to Delhi in the summar vacation. We alighted the train at Old Delhi Railway Station. We hired tonas and reached the Red Fort. Entry to the Fort was by tickets. Som,, we bought one for each and entered the Fort.

Just inside the gate, there is Nagar Khana. The imperial band played six times a day there. There were a few huge drums. Ahead, there was Diwan-i-Aam. Literally, it means place for the common man. It was here that the emperor used to hold his Darbar. It was from this place that he used to carry public business. He even received officers there. In short, it was the main centre for conducting government business.

After that is situated Diwan-i-Khas. Literally, it means place for the select few persons. It was, therefore, meant purely for private audience. Only the ministers could go there. It had a peacock throne. But, that was taken away by Nadir Shah. Even the Kohinorr was there. It is now in the crown of England. Beyond, there is the Rang Mahal. Literally, it means the building meant for enjoyment and recreation. In this building, there are beautiful baths known as Hamams. They were meant for royal bath. A part of this building is known as Zenana. It is because the ladies of the palace lived there.

The moti Masjid was reserved for the king to say his prayers. The museum was no less fascinating. Many kinds of Mughal dresses and weapons are at display there. It attracted a big crowd. Every person seemed to be very anxious to see everything closely.

There were all over lovely designs of paintings on the walls and the ceilings. The marble lotus was a great source of attraction. We came back after we were physically tired.

The memory of the visit still lingers in my mind. I wonder how great Shah Jahan was. He appears to be very fond of getting unique buildings built. The Red Fort bears good evidence to it.

IF I WERE THE PRINCIPAL OF MY SCHOOL

The principal has to manage every affair of the school. He plays the role of a polot in the smooth running of the school.

If I were the principal of my school, I would make the games compulsory for all the students. Sound mind can be found only in a sound body. I would work for the all-round development of the students.

I would arrange special classes for the weak students. I would inspect every class every month I would know how the teachers teach the students and check their home-work. I would be very careful about discipline. I would start pass-system. I shall punish the truants. I would see that the school is kept neat and clean. I would see that the library is well-maintained. The teachers would be given all possible facilities. I would see that the result of the school are toned up. I would also improve the quality of teaching and extra-curricular activities.

IF I WERE THE PRIME MINISTER OF MY COUNTRY

The Prime Minister is all in our country. He is the head of the government in a democratic country. He manages all the affairs of the country. He plays the role of a pilot in the smooth running of the country.

If I were the Prime Minister of India, I would dedicate my life to the service of humanity. I would give the country a planned economic development. I would remove poverty and unemployment. I would work to strengthen communal harmony. I woul curb terrorism.

I would punish hoarders, black-marketeers, adulterators, smugglers and bribery-seekers. I would give full freedom to press and courts. I would improve agriculture, transport and industries. I would check the rising prices.

THE DUSSEHRA

The Dussehra is an important festival of the Hindus. It generally falls during the month of October. Rama had killed Ravana on this day. This festival lasts for ten days. The Ramayana is staged every night. The people enjoy seeing Ram-Lila.

All the shops are decorated. The people buy sweets and crackers. Married girls get new clothes, money and sweets from their brothers and parents. Jhankis are taken out every day. The Dussehra fair attracts a huge crowd. The effigies of Ravana, Meghnath and Kumbhakaran are burnt. It marks the victory of the good over the evil. The people look cheerful. They make merry at night.

THE DEEPAWALI

Many festivals are celebrated in India, regularly every year. Holi, Diwali, Dushehra and Raksha Bandhan are the four great Hindu festivals. Though Diwali is celebrated by all the Hindus, it has a special significance for the Vaish community.

The festival is celebrated at the end of the rainy season and the beginning of the winter season. Sometimes, it takes place towards the end of October and at other times in the beginning of November. According to the Hindu calender, it falls every year in the month of Kartik. The season at this time is pleasant. It is neither too hot nor too cold.

The festival is celebrated in honour of the goddess Lakshmi, The Hindu goddess of wealth. It is believed that the goddess blesses those with prosperity, who keep their houses neat and clean on this day. The goddess is supposed to visit the Hindu homes at midnight.

Before the festival great preparations are made. Houses are white-washed and wells are cleaned. Furniture doors and windows are all polished and varnished. The walls are decorated with curtains and pictures. In every house sweets are prepared or purchased from the market. Sweets are exchanged among friends and relatives.

The day itself is marked with great rejoicing and merry-making. The illumination at night is a sight to see. There are rows of light, to be seen on the roof of every house and building Earthen lamps are lighted in large numbers. Many people now use multicoloured electric bulbs to illuminate their houses. The festival ends with the worship of goddess Lakshmi at about ten or eleven p. m. A picture or a small idol of the goddess is bathed in milk, prayers are offered and sweets are distributed.

The Hindu festival of light has many advantages. Houses are all cleaned and white washed on this occasion. The burning of sarson (mustard) oil purifies the atmosphere and kills insects that breed during the rainy season. It provides an occasion for merry-making for all. The children specially enjoy it. They get toys, sweets and delicious dishes to eat. I like this festival the most of all. Foreigners who have had occasion to enjoy it. have also prasied it highly. There is nothing to equal it in any country or religion.

HOLI

Holi is one of the biggest festivals of the Hindus. It takes place on the Purnima of the month of March every year. It is a spring festival. It is observed in every corner of the country without any distinction of caste, creed and colour.

Weeks before the festival, villagers sing, dance and play on various kinds of instruments. Women also dance and sing with men. Children and young men play different kinds of games. This goes on till late in the night. Nobody cares for the time or the cold.

On the festival day, special food is prepared. At night, men, women and children go to see Holika Dahan, singing, dancing and beating their drums.

Next day the people go out to meet and greet their friends and relations. They welcome one another with colours and gulal. It goes on till late in the noon. After noon, feasts are arranged. Friends are invited. The whole day is passed in merry-making and feasting.

This festival is of great importance. It strengthens social ties. But, some people misuse the occasion. Instead of `gulal' and `coloured water' they use mud, grease and other such dirty things. This often results in quarrels. Such misuse must be avoided.

I like this festival very much. It is a great festival of the Hindus. But, it should be celebrated in the proper way.

THE INDEPENDENCE DAY

15th August is a red letter day in the history of India. On this great day in 1947, India won back her freedom. We became marters of our own country. The English rule came to an end on this day. Since then we have been celebrating it as a historical day.

Our college celebrates independence day with great joy. This year we went to our college before sunrise. From there we went round the town streets for `Prabhat Pheri' or the happy morning round. We sang the songs to wake the sleeping people. We also sang songs of motherland. We shouted slogans and `Jai' of our motherland and of our great leaders.

At 8 o'clock in the morning we gathered in the school compound. The principal and teachers stood near the flag part. The N.C.C. Cadets in uniform stood in order in front of it. Other students stood behind them. The manager of the college hoisted the ``National Flag". As the flag was unforled flowers fell from it. The boys clapped joyfully. The N.C.C. cadets gave a salute. Five boys sand the National Anthem. All the people present stood at attention when the song was being sung.

Then same teachers read out the messages. There were sent by the Minister and the director of education. Some other teachers gave speeches. Some inispiring poems were also recited. The principal paid homage to the heroes and the fighters of freedom.

This day of Indendence brings us joy and hope. It again and again reminds us of our duty to the nation. It reminds us of the brave deeds and sacrifies of our great leaders who fought for us and won us freedom. It reminds us of Gandhi Ji, Sardar Patel, Nehru ji, Bhagat Singh, Subhash Chandra Bose, and others. It inspires us to follow them and make the country great. It tells us that no sacrifice is so great for the motherland.

THE REPUBLIC DAY

26th January is the Republic Day. It is a day of great national importance. On this day in 1950, the new constitution of India came into force. This new constitution declared India to be a sovereign democratic Republic. A Republic means a state in which authority of the government is derived from the people. The people of India are supreme and the government derives its power from the people. This day of national importance is celebrated every year.

This year the Republic Day was celebrated with great enthuiasm in our town. Volunteers in batches went out to Prabhat Pheri early in the morning before the day dawned. They moved from one street to another singing `Uth Jaag Musafir Bhor Bhai" the favourite song of Mahatma Gandhi. They called upon the people to get up and be ready to take part in the celebration.

At about 8 a. m. people assembled in the Ramlila ceremony. The chairman of the municipal committee unforled the flag amidest loud cheers. The military band played ``Jan Gan Man". The principal of the school delivered a speech on the importance of the day. Then the gathering broke up. All the students dispersed.

People spent the whole day in merry making. In the evening the markets and the street were tastefully decorated. Tricolour flags fluttered on the tops of buildings. At night the public buildings and markets will illuminated. We went to see the lights.

This day reminds us of our great leaders who had declared some years ago that their goal was complete freedom from the foreign rule. They converted their dream into reality when they gave us a constitituion on 26th January, 1950 and declared India to be sovereign Democratic Republic. Let us pledge that we would always observe the noble ideals contained in this constitution. Let us hope that our democracy will be a great succes in the years to came.

ADVANTAGES OF SCIENCE

Modern age is the age of science. The scientific inventions are playing a key role in the life of human society. Human life has become worth living in the present-day-world.

We owe Stephenson a lot for inventing the locomotive engine. As a result, railways are now playing an important part all over the world. The invention of the steam boat marked the beginning of the modern ship. The Wright Brothers were the first to fly successfully in the air.

Scientific inventions like electricity, Radio, cinema, wireless telegraphy, telephone etc. are very useful for us in our daily life. They give us great comfort and happiness. Science has proved to be a great blessing in agriculture, industry and in fields of medicine and surgery. Incurable diseases can now be cured with the help of science. It is a boon peace and a curse in war. It has given legs to the lame, ears to the deaf and eyes to the blind.

USES OF ELECTRICITY

Electricity is one of the chief organs of human life. It has magical powers. It influences our agriculture and industries. Electricity lights our stroots homes offices and factories. Its light is brighter than moon-light. It keeps our homes and factories warm or cool as we wish.

It can cook our food and wash our clothes. It can clean our rooms, cars and furniture like a slave. It has proved to be a boon in curing diseases or in finding out the defects. Television, telephone, telegram, and wireless speak high of its use.

Electricity provides power to trains and tram-cars. Electric cranes can shift heavy loads from one place to another. In this way, electricity is the most useful and wonderful discovery.

COMPUTER AND ITS USE

Computer is an electronic calculating machine. It works more or less human brain but more quickly. There are no chances of error if we operate it carefully. In the beginning it was simply a calculating machine doing addition, subtraction, division, and multiplication etc. But, now it helps in so many other ways also.

Now, computer is used in predicting the weather, in finding out the diseases and their treatments, in getting our seats and births reserved in train and finding out various datas and informations in factories, banks, L.I.C. Officers etc. It helps us in educational institutions also for checking the progress of students and in learning the work load of teacher. It works wonderfully in the field of astronomy and space travel.

In using computer we have to feed it with data and programmes. Then it gives us the answers and informations required. So its feeding or programme is the most important work because the reliability of our results defends upon our programme. So far feeding a computer specialist is needed. Then any man can handle it.

In foreign countries like Russia, America, and Japan many heavy electronic computers have been discovered. They will control the transport, trade, election and security arrangements. In India also we have started the use and manufacture of computers. Our present government is very keen to computerize the maximum number of services by the end of this centur. Its use will check the delay and corruption.

INVENTIONS OF SCIENCE

It is an age of science scientific inventions have made our lives easy and comfortable. They have made the world smaller.

Electricity is a boon to mankind. Electic bulbs and tubes light our homes, shopos, and streets. Electric fans and airconditioners give us cool air in summer. Heaters keep us warm in winter. Electriicty our machines-small and large. Domestic appliances like iron, mixer and grinder can be used only by electricity.

Machines serve as our extra limbs. They give us bodily pleasures. They save our time, energy, and labour.

Science has given easier and faster means of travelling at has brought a revolution in the field of agriculture. It has helped in the spread of education through the books printed on printing machines. Cinemas, radio and television have made our lives pleasant. Science has also saved humanity from many diseases which were considered incurable.

We have became slaves to science as we depend too much on it. Science has made us inactive also. Science has given us sane weapons. We are them to destroy mankind. So it is a bad master also.

All the glitters is not gold. Indeed science has made our lives worth living. Scientific inventions were made to serve us but they have became our master. So, it is true that science is a good servant but a bad master.

A CRICKET MATCH

Cricket is International game. I take a keen interest in cricket. Last year our school team played a cricket match against the team of Vidyawati Junior High School. A large crowd spectators gathered to watch the match.

I was selected in the school cricket team. Both the teams reached the play-ground at the right time, they were in their white uniforms.

The match started in time. The game teachers, Om Veer Singh and Mohd Aziz acted as umpires. Our Captain Ram Nath Sharma won the toss. He decided to bat first. He himself went as an opening batsman. Another opening batsman was Rajiv. Both the players played very well. They scored fifty runs. The captain Ram Nath was given run out by the Umpire. After his departure Rajiv could not stand for long. He was caught behind the wicketkeeper. The bowlers of the opposite team bowled so well that this whole team was out at two hundred runs only.

Now, our team took the field. The opposite team came to bat. I was incharge of the opening bowler. Our bowlers bowled so decently that the batsmen of this opposite team were dismissed one after another. The whole team was out at one hundred eight runs only. They lost the match by three runs as our team made One hundred ten.

In this way our team was declared victorius. Everybody praised our captain who batted as well as bowled very well. The captain of this opposite team tried his beat to turn the game into draw but he could not do so.

RAINY DAY

It was saturday morning a gentle breeze was blowing from the cart. It started drizzling after sometime. It was school time. So, I left home for school with my friend Mohan. On our way to school it started raining cats and dogs. All over clothes and books got wet. We reached our school after half an hour.

It was still raining heavily. The rooms were in complete darkness. We saw that very few teachers and the students were present. The attendance was very poor. Seeing this principal declared it a rainy day holiday. All the boys began to dance with joy. After sometime the rain stopped. My friend and I started for home.

There was rain water everywhere on the road. The pools were full of water. Animals and birds were swimming in the water. Children ran here and there and played joyfully in the water. Crown up people are also enjoyed a rain bath. The people flet comfort after the heat of summer. Nature presented a beautiful right. Frogs began to crook loudly. The weather became very pleasant.

After reaching home I took rest for sometime. My mother prepared tea. I took tea and sandwiches. Then I went out. My younger brother also accompanied me. We enjoyed natural scenery very much. We returned home in the evening feeling happy.

HOLIDAYS

There is not much need of proving to most school boys that holidays are necessary. They are quite convinced that they are and most desirable too. The welcome a holiday from school with hilarious joy, and plague the headmaster on the least excuse to let them off their lessons. It would be more in place to try to convince them of the neccesity of work and study. Yet it may be desireable to show that regular intervals of rest, recreations, or change of occupation are really necessary. As the old rhyme says :

"All work and no play,
makes jack a dull boy."

Holidays at proper intervals are especially necessary for young people and for there engaged in hard mental work; for continuous work, without a break, will injure the health and may came a nervous break down. A short holiday, rightly used, will send us back to our work with renewed zest and vigour.

``Rightly used". It all depends upon that. For holidays may be abused. If the holiday is spent in s tupid idleness, or in an exhausting round of exciting amusements, or shut up in clore stuffy rooms drinking and playing, or in any other unhealthy way the boy or man will come back to his work tired, and unintrested. The holidays, instead of doing good, has done harm. much more harm than steady work could ever do.

How can a holiday, then, be but used, so that at the end of it we shall came back to our work with energies renewed and interest keener than ever ? If we are students or have been shut up in stuffy offices, we should yet away into the pure air of the country and live a healthy open air life, enjoying games or sports. We should avoid unhealthy amusements keep early hours and get plenty of refreshing sleep. And we should not be completely idle. Change of occupation is a rest. ANd if we have a little regular work to do, work that we take an interest in, it will make our holiday not only healthier but more enjoyable.

EXAMINATION

We live in an age of examinations. Students have to face examinations right from childhood. Even the sweet, innocent toddler seeking admission to the K. G. Class is not spared. Thus, examinations in our educational system have assumed an importance out of all proportion to their actual educational value. Our school, and colleges are no longer seats of learning and enlightenment but are only examining and promoting bodies turning out young degree holders in their thousands. The chief anxiety of a student is not how to study but how to prepare for and pass his examination and that of the teacher is not how to teach or what to teach but how to coach his pupils for their examinations. A school is judged not by its overall contribution to all round progress of its pupils but by its examination results.

Because of their exaggerated importance, examinations have become a veritable nightmare for our pupils. The whole career of a pupil depends on his performance in the examination hall. If for any reason he cannot appear for the examination, he has to lore a whole year examinations are a game of chance. If the question happen to be the ones he has anticipated, he is lucky to pass. If they are in family he is doomed to fail, assessment standard being subjective, varies from examiner to examiner. Even in the care of the same examiner, if sometimes depends upon his mood.

Our examinations put a premium as memory. The encourage cramming students hunt about for likely questions and manage to pass the examination by hook or crook.

The end products of there unreliable examinations are only degree holders and job hunters, not learned and cultured citizens. We need to overhaul the entire present system of examinations in the best interest of our students. Mass examination and mass amusement must be scrapped forthwith. The element of chance must be eliminated as much as possible.

Lastly, the degree job nexus must be ended. Those who do not want to persue higher studies and instead want to take up jobs, should be provided both in job and out of the job training which would help them to achieve the skill and the knowledge necessary for the job and get promotion.

THE SCHOOL MAGAZINE

Every good school has its good magazine. It is brought out once a year. It is managed by special magazine committee. This commitee consists of a couple of teachers and few bright pupils who have a flair for writing. One of the teachers or pupils becomes the editor of the magazine.

The magazine committee invites and receives articles, stories, poems, cartoons, photographs and reports about the school activities from the students and teachers. It carefully selects and finalises the matter. Then it gets the magazine printed and distributed. The magazine contains the principal's annual report, a diary of the school activiites and the photographs of the school staff and students association. The pride of place goes to the scholars and sport champions who have brought pride and glory to the school.

The school magazine is very important and useful part of the activities of the school. It encourages students to read a lot and contribute their but in the form of written matter to the magazine. It develop it develops their creative talents. It provides them a medium for free and artistic self expression. It gives them administrative experience and sense of responsibility and cultivates a team spirit. It gives the students a sense of belonging to the school. It makes the students more involved and interested in all the activities of the school and raise the academic standard of pupi in general. Thus the school magazine promotes the formation of character and personality. The pupils love to see and read their contributions in print. They consider themselves to be budding writers. They ye a wonderful thrill out of this creative experience. The school magazine gives healthy and deserve publicity to its outstanding students. It brings to the notice of the outside world, the strihing features of this school. It is also an annual record of the school highlighting the achievements and landmarks in the school history. We can evaluate the standard of a school from its magzine.

MY SCHOOL MEMORIES

Having left school behind me finally and for ever. I often find memories of my school life flashing back on my mind. How clearly vividly, do I remember my first day at school ! It was a day that dawned with mixed feelings of loneliness and fear, uncertainty and anxiety, curiousity and excitement. And it ended with very pleasant feelings of mental relief and joy. I recall my first teacher, an exceptionally kind, sympathetic and good-humoured man. On my first entry, he welcomed me into his class warmly. He taught us so well that I found everything simple, easy and interesting. My initial fright of school disappeared. And, then, I recollect my last day at school, a day of farewell speeches and painful parting. On that day I realised that parting can be a sweet sorrow.

Now the memory of an unforgettable experience leaps into my mind. I was at that time in the seventh standard. One day I was on my way have from school. Suddenly, a boy ran up to me from behind and accosted me. I knew him, for he had asked me to write up his home work and naturally. I had refuse to oblige him. He caught me unawares and showed me into a nearby pool of muddy water. There was mud all over me which made me look like frightful figure. Fortunately, for me, same of my class master were passing by. They saw my plight. They hired a richshaw and took me home. The next morning the mischief margercame to my place and tendered an apology. He requested me not to report the matter to the headmaster who was known to be strict. He said he came from poor family and if he was dismissed from the school, it would came as a great shock to his parents. They would be very miserable. I sympathised with him and promised not to complain. Since then we have been very good friends. He is grateful to me for my act of magnanimity that saved him his school career.

All our teachers taught us well. They took a lot of pains for us and guided us patiently and wisely. The principal, though a strict disciplinarian, was large hearted and broad minded. I made many lasting friends at school. I remember them all when I think about my school days. I cherish the memories of my schoo days and often enjoy reliving there wonderful times

HEALTH IS WEALTH

Everybody will agree that health is w ealth. The saying means that health is the most valuable thing in the world.

Though health is no doubt wealth, it would be more appropriate to say that it is better then wealth If we have to choose between health and wealth, we would unheritatingly choose health, for wealth withou health is of no use. But, health without would be sufficient to lead a happly life. Health and wealth are the two most essential conditions of happiness but of there two health is the necessary condition while wealth is only a desirable condition. I health man can, if he tries, get wealth, but a wealthy man without health may not succeed in gaining his lost health. So, health is by itself wealth. It is in any case, perferable to wealth.

There are many rich men whose only ambition in life has been to make money. They work day in and day out and succeed within a few years in realizing their ambition. They become rich. But, at what cost ? The fast tempo of their life and their unnatural life style ruin their health. Many of them suffer from a number of ailments like high blood pressure, ulcer, diabetes and heart trouble. They go there only at night to sleep for a few hours. They can have the choicest meals but alas ! they cannot digest them. They have not time for their family members and friends. They have the wealth to secure all the pleasures of life, but they have no capacity to enjoy them. Many of them became physical wrecks and either die prematurely or lie the rest of their lives in bed within the four walls of a running room.

In contrast, a healthy body can enjoy all the pleasures of life. Though a healthy man may not be able to secure pleasures resulting from luxuries, he can enjoy simple pleasures of life which make for happiness for happiness lies not in in luxurious living but in small, simple enjoyments of life. A brisk walk in the morning, a dip in the sea or swimming pool, a game or two in open, a hearty meal and sound sleep give us happiness which no luxury can give.

Besides, our mental facilities are also close connected with our body. A sound mind in a sound body. Our mind can be active and creative only if our body is healthy. If we have a healthy body and healty mind, wealth is not far away. Though wealth, at its best is but a means to happiness. A healthy body and healthy are a permanent source of happiness and therefore, be called the greatest items of wealth be prized.

NEWSPAPERS

Newspapers form an essential part of modern civilization. To many of us our morning tea would lore its flavour if it is not accompanied by a newspaper.

Any printed matter whose chief function is to supply news is called a newspaper. But, we usually refer only to a daily as a newspaper. The new information which comes from North, East, West and South is called news. It has some element of novelty. For example, it is said that if a dog bites a man, it is not news but if a man bites a dog, it is news.

Though the primary function of a newspaper is to supply news. It also provides information on a variety of subjects like government, politics, science, art business, sports, crimes, fashions, health, childcare, food, travel, important social and religious events etc. in the forms of news cr feature articles. Most of the newspapers also have advice columns, readers, views, columns, comic strips, crossword puzzles, astrological forecasts and various entertainment features.

The newspapers are called the eyes and ears of the world. They keep people in all parts of the world well informed of the latent developments through out the world. They provide latent news information about the developments in all branches of knowledge, investigate and present important events, guide and mould public opinion, serve as a medium for the ventilation of public grievance serve as an instrument of social reformation and educate people in citizenship. They act as a medicine of communication between the people and the government. The country is said to have a free press if the newspaper are free from government control and interference. Free press is not only the best safeguard for democracy, but also the essential condition of democracy. The very foundation in which democracy rests and flourishes.

In our country we are conversant with the crudsades of the press against corruption, against the social evils life sati, and against government restriction on the press. We have seem how powerful investigation conducted by the leading dailies have expored even the corrupt ministers and around public indignation to such an extent that same of the ministers and even Chief Minister are forced to step down. So, powerful and effective is the influence of newspapers on public opinion that the press is called the fourth estate.

FRIENDSHIP

There is a line in a song Shakespear's play `As You Like It', at says `Most friendship is feigning, most loving mere fully. This is most true sincere friendship is very rare. In most cases friendship is false. Our common friends are mostly fair weather friends. They are with us as long as we are rich and happy. They share our prosperity and pleasure. They do not stand by us when we need them most.

We know the story of the two friends who were passing through a forest.. When a bear was seen, the stranger and more active of the two deserted his companion and scrambled up a tree. The other man lay down as if dead. The bear sniffed them all over, then went away taking him to be dead. The false friend came down and asked what the bear had said in his ear. The angry man got up and told him that the bear had asked him not to trust selfish and imincere companions. This is what we often experience in our lives. When we are in dire need of our friends help, we find that he has vanished.

It is said that propsperity gains friends, adversity tries them. True friends do not desert us when we are in difficulties. They stand by us through thick and thin and do whatever they can to help us. There is the selfers and self sacrificing friendship.

How many men are prepared to make sacrifice for their friends. Hardly any `Laugh', and the world laughs with you : weep and you weep alone `says a wise man". We realize the truth of this saying when we are in trouble. But we do not like false, fear weather friends we should on our part try to be honest and faithful to our friends. We should always be friends in need and thus friends indeed.

HANDSOME IS THAT HANDSOME DOES

The literal meaning of the word `Handsome is of fine form or figure. A handsome person is good looking person, a person with pleasing looks. We always like to meet such persons. If we are ourselves handsome, we are thrilled to see other less fortunate people delighted when they meet us. Beauty is always bewitching. The poet Keats was right when he s aid, ``A thing of beauty is a joy for ever." Conversely, the person who is not handsome does not attract us and the ugly looking individual repels us.

But there is something more to handome looks or to beauty than mere outwardly pleasing appearance. Suppose a very handsome man commits murder. Would any of us he pleased to meet him ? Would his looks still delight us ? Certainly not physical beauty is no real beauty unless internal beauty emanates from it. To be truely beautiful is not only to look pretty physically but be handsome by virtue of good and noble deeds. Handsome is that handsome does. Suppose a very ugly man risks his own life and saves a boy from getting drowned. Would be still look ugly to us ? No, his inner beauty will appeal to us and will thrill us with joy. Though ugly in looks, he is handsome to our eyes because of his handsome deeds.

Mahatma Gandhi did not have physical beauty. But he ever repel anyone. He actually won the hearts of millions throughout the world why ? Became the beauty of his soul blazed forth through his good and great selfish thoughts, words and deeds. He had the most winning smile in the world though he was toothless. Though ordinary in appearance, he was really handsome.

So, we can be really handsome, if and only if our thoughts, words and deeds are handsome. We can never do handsome deeds unless our thoughts, too, are handsome and if our thoughts are handsome, we cannot do dirty things or speak dirty words. We cannot be truly and wholy handsome unless we are handsome externally as well as internally. Inner beauty blooms, through good deeds, accompanied by good thoughts and words. Thus, it is that handsome is that handsome does.

A HEROINE FROM INDIAN HISTORY

The heroine of Indian History I like most is Maharani Lakshmi Bai of Jhansi. She was born on November 1, 1835, at Kashi (Varansi). She received her early education with her cousin Nana Sahib, the son of Baji Rao. She was very much interested in horse-riding and other arts of warfare.

She was married at the age of fourteen to Gangadhar Rao, the Raja of Jhansi. He has about 50 years old at the time. But alongwith Raja Gangadhar Rao Lakshmi Bai was married to the throne of Jhansi also. Now, she became Maharani Lakshmi Bai of Jhansi.

During her married life at Jhansi, she took been interest in the fine arts as well as in military training. She knew the evil designs of the British Government very well. The English rulers refused to recognise their adopted son. Soon after the adoption of Damodar Rao and the declaration that he was the heir to the throne of Jhansi, among the other Indian rulers.

There is no other parallel in Indian History to Maharani Lakshmi Bai. No sacrifice was too great for her for the sake of her motherland. Had there been few other fighters like Rani of Jhansi, our country would have been free long, long ago. Her last wish at the time of her death was that no English Man should touch her body. She was the bravest of all the brave fighters for freedom.

THE SUMMER SEASON

India is indeed a continent. Here season is not the same throughout the country. When it is hottest in the plains, Kullu, Manali, Mussoorie and Darjeeling are very cold. When there is winter in west coast of India heavy rain falls on the coast of coromandal.

The Indian summer is the hottest season in the whole of year. The rays of the sun fall perpendicularly. Hence it is difficult to walk in the day. At midday we do not like to go out of doors because the heat is intense. The light is blinding in the day. We can do a little work only in the morning. The rich people make use of electric fans and coolers. Generally the greater part of the day is wasted. Sometimes it is very close. We drink glass of water again and again.

School and College hours are changed during summer. All institutions work in the morning. They are closed for all the summer. All educational offices work only upto noon. All offices and some of big shops use Khuskhus curtains. Chiks and curtains are used nearly in every house. They are kept wet during the day.

Small rivers, ponds and tanks go dry in the season. There is scarcity of water everywhere. The water in the wells sink low. Cattle find grazing grounds dry. The grass becomes withered and insufficient. Hence cattle quench their thirst with muddy and foul water.

Summer is the season of best fruits in our country. Mangoes, watermelons, Aru, Oranges and other tasty fruits come in the market. These fruits quench our thirst during this dry season.

The days are long. The heat goes on increasing till the afternoon. Even the sunset fails to give relief. Hot wind still goes on. It is after 8 o'clock at night that there is a little coolness. People generally sleep in the open space. Fans work to give us relief.

WINTER MORNING

Winter morning has its own beauty. One does not like to get out of the bed. But one can enjoy better in the open. Morning walk in winter is a fine treat. One winter morning I decided to go for a walk. Very cold breeze was blowing. I had to cover my face, my ears with a muffler. I put my hands in my pockets. My eyes were watery and my feet were cold. I saw a very few people on the roads. But all of them were wrapped up in woollen clothes. It was difficult to recognise anyone. Even animals like rabbits, dogs were hiding in the bushes of the garden. No bird was chirping. There was mist all around. Nothing was visible. From a distance even trees looked like ghosts. Similarly, cars on the roads were not visible. Waking in such an atmosphere has a pleasure of its own. After sometime one does not shiver and enjoys the cold.

Winter mornings are calm and quiet. I was not disturbed by any noise. People do not stir out. Birds remain in their nests. But summer mornings are noisy. In summer you came across many old people coughing and sneezing. Birds also chirp in summer. Winter morning is more refreshing. The winter wind gives a new thrill. Rising sun during winter is the best scene of nature. We see monkeys and birds sitting on the trees and waiting for the sunrise. I like winter mornings more than summer mornings.

THE SPRING SEASON

Spring is the most pleasant season in India. In this season everybody feels happy after the intense cold of winter. All take interest in outdoor life. The earth wears a green dress. Again it comes to life.

In this season the nature is kind. It gives us pleasure and joy. The trees, once more look fresh and lovely. They regain their lost leaves. The birds were silent in winter. Now they sing songs. They thank God with their thousands of notes. Nature gives a grand feast to our hundry eyes. It invites us to come out and take part in the joy of the world. It present a lovely sight for our hungry eyes. We get new strength from the kind mother of nature. The cool breeze invite us to come into the open. Buds of flowers peep to see the beautiful sight of nature. Flowers spread their sweet smell in all directions. They fill us with pleasure.

The pleasures of the spring are many. We cannot describe them. We can enjoy them in a village. There nature is in a naked form. Go to the mountain. There the nature is in its true colour. There everything is untouched by the dirty hand of man. In towns and cities calendar tells the coming offspring. But in villages every thing tells of its arrival. Open green fields present lovely scene to our tired eyes. The people of great cities like Mumbai and Calcutta can hardly know the glory of spring, the king of seasons.

Trees in spring present beautiful feast to our eyes. The sight of green and yellow fields fill our hearts with hope. The fields promise to give us corn. This lovely season fills us with the feeling of gratitude to God. We pray to God, the creator of spring. The solitude in the lap of a forest and a cave on a mountain present beauties of spring before our eyes. Spring is the season in which the voice of nature is heard everywhere.

GAMES AND SPORTS

Games and sport are an important factor in education. In the past there was no provision for them in Indian schools and colleges. But now no educational institution is complete without some arrangement for different games and sports. They improve health and help in building up a good body. As games are played in the open air, the body gets plenty of sunshine and fresh air.

The value of good health is well expressed in the proverb "A sound mind in a sound body." Games have another advantage. They develop a sprint of comradeship. Students do not play for themselves only but for the team as a whole. Thus a sportsman develops a broad outlook and learns the value of co-operative work. These habits prove highly useful in life. Players learn to obey their captain and carry out his instructions. And one who learns to obey also learns to command. Those who becomes captains develop qualities of leadership. Such training is as important as the study of books. Games often help in entering life. A good player is generally preferred to a bookworm with no interest in games. Extraordinary players choose games as their profession in life. Sometimes they are selected to represent their country in international tournaments or Olympic Games.

Games are necessary, but only as a help in keeping fit for carrying out our daily work. Too much cultivation of games has harmful result.

PHYSICAL EXERCISES

Life is a great struggle in many ways. Man has to fight against disease, poverty, misfortunes and so many other troubles. The best way to fight these strong enemies is to possess a sound health. Thus physical fitness is the first duty of all men. Proper and regular exercise is one of the best means to attain physical fitness. Some people believe that medicine and tonic maintain sound health. No mistake can be greater than this belief. Tonics and medicine provide temporary energy. Real and lasting energy cannot be got from them. It is physical training alone that can make us healthy and energetic. It is a cure for almost all bodily ills and weaknesses. Physical culture i.e., proper development of the body, has become a regular science. Even the greatest doctors of the world admit that certain chronic diseases like constipation or asthma can be cured only through physical exercise and medical treatment. Even bad eyesight is restored to normal through certain exercises for the eye. Many Indian 'Asans' are famous for their healthy effects on the human body.

It is difficult to discuss the value of physical fitness. Its importance for the individual has already been pointed out. But its value for the nation is even greater. Today India needs strong and healthy citizens to guard her newly won freedom. She has her enemies. Only if her people are strong she can preserve her freedom. We should not forget that a nation of weaklings is doomed to be the slave of others.

Physical health is useful in every walk of life. For example, great intellectual achievements are not possible, without good health. "A sound mind in a sound body" is a well-known saying. Again a sound body does not mean a sturdy body like that of Gama. To conclude, physical fitness is both a necessity and a blessing.

IMPORTANCE OF TRAVELLING

We travel for business. We travel for sight seeing. We travel for necessity. But a very few in our country travel to acquire knowledge. In Europe travelling is a necessary part of education. Educational value of travelling can hardly be described. Bacon says that travelling in younger age is a part of education, in the elder a part of experience. Travelling teaches us better than books. Sense organ is not very powerful factor. The eye is very essential in learning. We read of the existence, in the past, of a university called Nalanda. They say that there were one hundred lecture rooms. We think this a fact of imagination. Run to this spot. Your doubt will at once be removed.

Travelling is essential for the healthy growth of mind. "The mind's health." Says Rabinranath Tagore, "Cannot be maintained on the ration supplied by books in our class rooms." Travelling broadens our outlook. It makes us liberal in thought and outlook. It deepens our sympathies. The experience enables us to see things from a new angle of vision. It develop us a correct sense of value. Travelling brings us closer to nature. To a traveller nature becomes a living thing. It speaks in a language more impressive than any pen can make. It is very essential that students should have every chance of travel. Our schools and colleges should make arrangement for funds. The railway authorities should issue very cheap tickets for students to give chance to travel.

To take the full advantage of travelling we must have eyes to see, ears to listen and a desire to learn.

MY DAILY ROUTINE

I am a student of fourth class. Hence my daily life follows a very simple routine. I once heard from my teacher that early rising is the father of three blessings-health, wealth and wisdom. Since then I have been rising early in the morning. I get up at 4 O' clock. After doing my morning duties. I take bath in fresh water. I put on my clean clothes and go to the nearby temple. It is my grandmother's wish that I should begin the day's work with a prayer to God. Then I take my breakfast. It consists of a few biscuits and a glass of milk. Then I sit at my books. I read them till 7.30 a.m. During two hours I practically finish all the reading of my lessons. Then I complete the home work of different subjects. I do not believe in eleventh hour preparations. I known that labour will lead to success.

The school begins at 8.30 a.m. I am at school fifteen minutes earlier. I take much interest in the school work.

The school breaks up at 2.30 p.m. I return home at about 3.00 p.m. Having taken the light lunch I take rest for an hour. At 4.30 p.m. I complete the home work. At 5.30 p.m. I go to pay cricket or badminton. Here I spend an hour. My body begins to perspire. Then I get back home and take a cold bath. Now, I feel myself light. After having my dinner I take evening walk. Then I sit by the side of my mother. She tells me good stories. At about 9.30 p.m. I go to bed. On Sunday, I sometimes go to relatives house for entertainment. At other times I go to visit my friends. In holidays there is a break in the daily routine. But, I never break the golden rule of "early to bed and early to rise."

A DOCTOR

A Doctor is a very important in society. It is the Doctor who looks after the sick and suffering and brings relief to them. Without him the sick would continue to suffer, and they would die ultimately.

A Doctor is a very busy man. He works day and night. He goes to his clinic early in the morning. If he is employed in some hospital he goes to the hospital. Patients are always waiting for him. he at once begins his works. He examines them one after another. h carries with him his stethoscope with which he examine the chest of the patient. If this way, he finds out if they ar suffering from any ling or heart trouble. Havin examined them thoroughly, he writes the prescription He also tells them what food they should take and wha other precautions are necessary.

A good Doctor is sweet tempered. He knows that th patient is ill and anxious about his health, and so he i very patient in dealing with him. He does not get irritated He is sympathetic and kind, and does his best for the sick

Our country has made rapid progress in the medica field. A number of medical colleges have been opened al over the country and Doctors are being turned out in larg numbers. Still there is shortage of Doctors in the villages Also there is overcrowding in the hospitals. Muc improvement is necessary.

THE BOOK I LIKE MOST

Of all the books I have read, I like the 'Ramcharitr Manas', best. Sri Goswami Tulsi Das is the writer of thi epic. Every Indian has read or heard the story Ram an Sita. This popular story has been narrated in this book i the most beautiful way. We are told in it first the reason for the birth of Lord Rama. On the insistence of variou gods and goddesses he came on the earth in the form of human being to relieve the pain and suffering of th virtuous. The book is divided into various parts. Every part deals with a particular aspect of the life or performance of lord Rama.

All the Hindus accept it as a great religious book. It lays down the rules of conduct for all. It make everyone believe that the virtuous are always protected by the Lord. How Ravana, the symbol of evil, was defeated is well known to all. How the creator of all, Lord Rama, showered his love on every who had a firm in him, becomes evident from this book. The stories of poor old Bhilni, Shabri, and Boatsman, "Kavet", support this statement. Indeed, as a religious book it cannot be surpassed by any other.

One book may be good from one point of view. Another one may be good from some other points of view. It is my philosopher and guide. I always like to read it.

THE SEASONS OF INDIA

There are four seasons that are common to the whole of India. They are the summer the rainy season, the winter, and the spring.

The Summer Season begin from the month of April and lasts upto the end of June. The sun shines at its brightest and there is intense heat People perspire all over. In the day, hot winds, called '100', blow and many die of heat stroke. People like to wear their white clothes.

Kurtas of mulmul are the popular articles of clothes in this season. While at home, people like to remain half naked. Punkahs are used by all. The season is a lazy one. People do not like to work. Hence it is that all schools and colleges are closed during these months. Melons, watermelons, cucumbers, etc., are the special fruits of this season.

The rains are most welcome after the intense heat and dryness of the summer months. The people heave a sight of relief as the rainy season begin and the first showers fall. The timely arrival of rains is most essential for an agricultural country like India, where the success or failure crops depends upon rains. The rain washes down all dust from trees and plants and all nature appears green and beautiful. It is pleasant to take long walks or to go out on pincincs. Sometimes when the rains are heavy there are floods in the rivers of the country, causing much death and destruction. The mango, the King of fruits, is the special of this season. Young and old, rich and poor, all like to enjoy the fruit.

The rainy season is followed by the winter. This is the healthiest part of the year. People feel active and like to work. Woolen clothes, suits, pullovers etc., are used to keep off the cold. The people like to bask in the sun in the day and to warm themselves by the fire in the evenings and nights. Those who can afford them use electric heaters to heat their rooms. This is the season of plenty. A large number of vegetables and fruits grow is abundance and even the poor can eat them as they are cheap.

The spring, the golden season, in whose praise so much has been written comes after winter. It begins with the 'Basant Panchmi' early in February and continues to the end of March. It is the season when all the trees and plants are in bloom, when the crops ripen and the fields are golden as far as the eye can see. Nature is at its best during the season. The trees are tall clothed with new and bright leaves. It is green everywhere. It is neither too hot nor too cold. People enjoy going on picnics. Spring is a season of reveling and merrymaking. The spring revels reach a climax during the Holi festival in March. There is not but colour everywhere.

Such are different seasons of India.

RIVERS OF INDIA

Some of the rives of India are world famous. In the North, we have the Ganges, the Yumana, the Brahmputra and their numerous branches. The Ganges is regarded as sacred by the Hindus. They call it 'Ganga Mata'. In the south, Krishna, Kaveri, Narbda and Tapti, etc., are very famous. many of our big cities are situated on the banks of these rivers. They are important places of pilgrimage, for example, Allahabad, Haridwar and Banaras.

We are rightly proud of our rivers. Some of them have made world famous fertile lands. They have been depositing good alluvial sand year after year. In this way, the Ganges and Yamuna rivers support life on the plains.

The rivers help us to irrigate our fields. Canals have been dug out of the rivers and they supply water to the farmers. Thus the progress and success of our agriculture is closely linked up with the rivers.

In ancient times were a good source of transport. In our times also they are used for transport. Large wood logs are carried by them from the mountain to the plains with the flow of water. Boats and steamers also help in carrying passengers and goods on the rivers.

Rivers help in generating power. They help in the breeding of fishes. Rivers are also a good source of picnics and enjoyment.